This Is a Let's-Read-and-Find-Out Science Book®

I'm Growing!

by Aliki

HarperCollins*Publishers*

for
Alene Kellogg Rhea

and for
David, Faviola, and Eric Lomale

The *Let's-Read-and-Find-Out Science Book* series was originated by Dr. Franklyn M. Branley, Astronomer Emeritus and former Chairman of the American Museum—Hayden Planetarium, and was formerly co-edited by him and Dr. Roma Gans, Professor Emeritus of Childhood Education, Teachers College, Columbia University. For a complete catalog of Let's-Read-and-Find-Out Science Books, write to HarperCollins Children's Books, 10 East 53rd Street, New York, NY 10022.

Let's-Read-and-Find-Out Science Book is a registered trademark of HarperCollins Publishers.

The illustrations for this book
were done on watercolor board using
ink, watercolors, and pencil crayons.

I'm Growing!   Copyright © 1992 by Aliki Brandenberg   Typography by Christine Kettner

Library of Congress Cataloging-in-Publication Data   Aliki.   I'm growing! / by Aliki.
p.   cm. — (Let's-read-and-find-out science book)
Summary: Describes human growth and how the different parts of the body change as it grows.
ISBN 0-06-020244-0. — ISBN 0-06-020245-9 (lib. bdg.)   1. Human growth — Juvenile literature.
2. Children — Growth — Juvenile literature.   [1. Growth.]   I. Title.   II. Series.
QP84.A44   1992   612.6'5 — dc20   91-14087   CIP   AC

1 2 3 4 5 6 7 8 9 10   First Edition

I'm Growing!

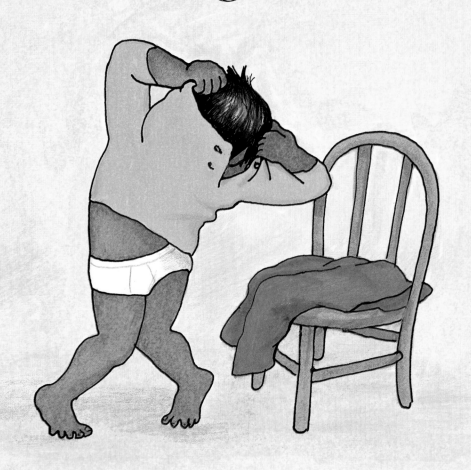

Look at me!
My clothes don't fit.
My shirt won't button.
My jeans are too short.
The waist doesn't snap.
My shoes are too tight.
My cap won't go on.

I'm growing!

I have been growing for a long time.
Here is a picture of me when I was a baby.
I can't believe how little I was!

Look how I've grown

and grown

and grown.

I look different now.
The features of my face have changed.
They are bigger—especially my nose.

My arms and legs are longer.
So are my body and my neck.
I am heavier and taller.

While I have been growing on the outside,
I've been growing inside, too.
My bones are bigger.
My muscles are bigger.

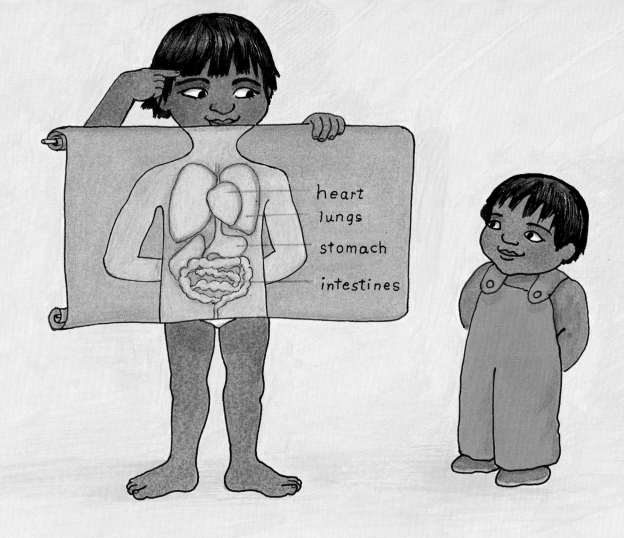

heart
lungs
stomach
intestines

So are my brain, my heart, my lungs, my stomach, and my other organs.

And while everything inside me grows,
the skin that covers me grows, too.
No matter how big your bones get,
your skin will always fit.
You may pop your buttons,
but you can't pop your skin!

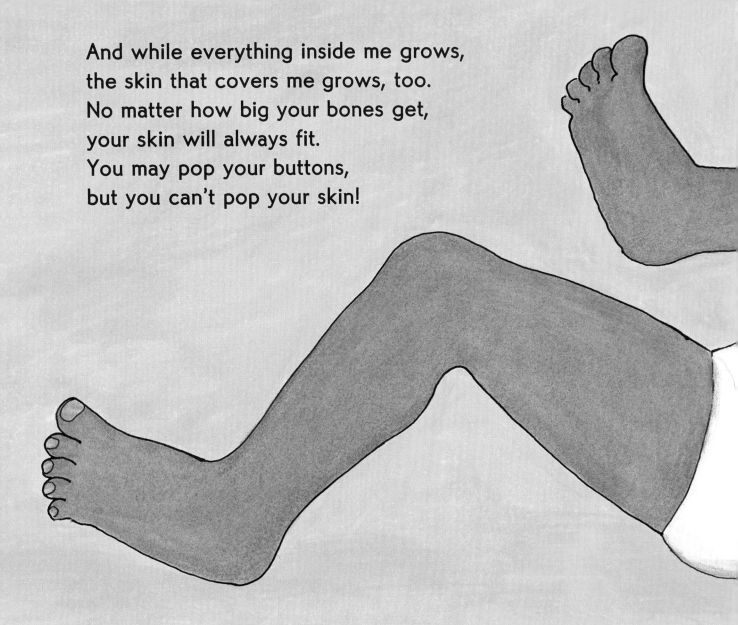

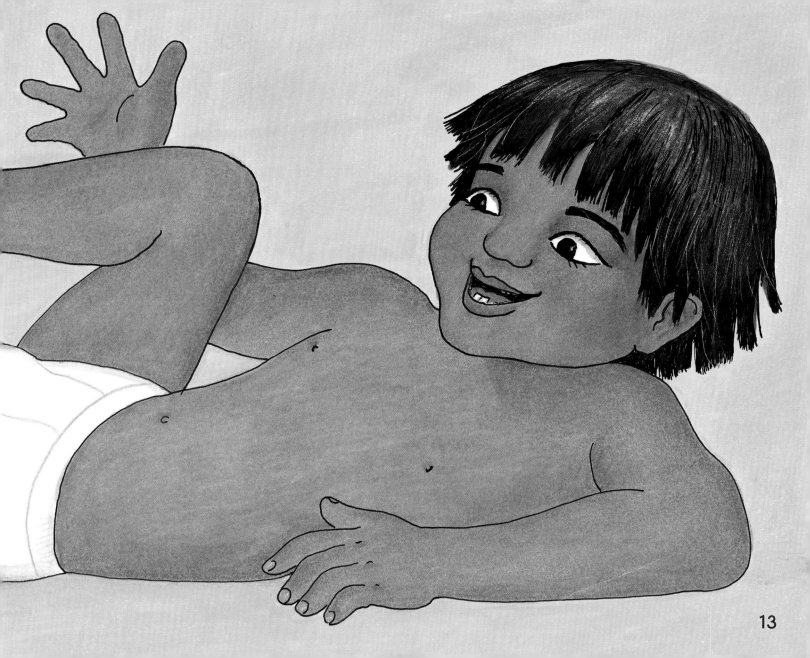

When I was a baby, I had baby teeth.
Now I am losing my baby teeth.
My new teeth are bigger.
They will fit my growing face.

I have to take care of my new teeth.
They have to last me all my life.

Most people grow until they reach a certain age.
But sometimes, something goes wrong.
For some reason, a person may grow very little,
or stop growing too soon.
That's what happened to our friend.
He remained small even though he is a grown-up.

17

Most people stop growing in their late teens.
After that, a person may grow thinner or fatter.

And everyone grows older.
But bones and organs don't grow bigger anymore.

Yet some parts of you don't stop growing.
Hair is always growing.
Look at Anna's.
Anna has never cut her hair.
She can almost sit on it.

Louie's hair grows fast.
He gets a haircut every month.

Jenny's grandfather has lost the hair
on top of his head.
But it keeps growing around the sides.

Fingernails and toenails
never stop growing, either.

21

When you play, you use up energy.
When you grow, you use up energy, too.
That's why you get hungry.

Food—especially good food, with proteins
and vitamins and minerals in it—
gives you energy.
It helps you grow.

I eat a good breakfast and a good lunch.
When I come home from school, I'm hungry again.
I have a snack.
Then I have a good dinner.
I tell my mother I'm a growing boy.

Not everyone eats the same amount.
Right now I eat more than my big sister
or my little brother.
But they are growing, too.

Not everyone grows at the same time, either.
Some people grow in spurts.
I took a picture with my friends last year.
Look at us now.
Our sizes have changed.
Yet we are all the same age.

We are all growing in our own way,
at our own speed.
When we are all grown up,
we may be the same size.

Or we may end up different sizes.

Right now I am my size, and I am going
to try on my new clothes.

They are a little big, but I'll grow into them.

It will happen to you, too.